NICK FAWCETT

Poems to help you *Pray*

kevin mayhew

First published in 2006 by

KEVIN MAYHEW LTD
Buxhall, Stowmarket, Suffolk, IP14 3BW
E-mail: info@kevinmayhewltd.com
www.kevinmayhew.com

9 8 7 6 5 4 3 2 1 0

ISBN 978 1 84417 717 2
Catalogue No. 1500968

Cover design by Sara-Jane Came
Edited and typeset by Katherine Laidler

Printed and bound in Great Britain

Contents

THANKSGIVING

INTERCESSION

Introduction

Do you like poetry? In my experience some love while others loathe it, and I can well understand both points of view. Rhyming poems can be banal or embarrassingly simplistic, completely failing to touch us. Equally, blank verse can be so obscure and subjective that, however often we read it, we have no idea what the author is trying to say. Clearly, then, poetry has its pitfalls.

On the other hand, we grow up with poems from an early age in the form of nursery rhymes, many of which we'll remember for the rest of our lives. As Christians, we grow up, in terms of worship, with another form of poetry: namely hymns, a good number of which we'll similarly always remember. Although their rhyme and rhythm may not consciously register, it resonates deep within, sticking in the mind and offering a unique source of inspiration, comfort, challenge or guidance. It's this that led me, some time ago, to explore poetry as a medium of prayer, and the result was a set of four gifts books together with a number of hymn texts, all published by Kevin Mayhew. In this book, I've pulled those together and supplemented them with new material to provide a resource for personal or public devotion. The 104 poems collected here are grouped under five headings – praise and worship, confession and forgiveness, thanksgiving, petition (prayers for ourselves) and intercession (prayers for others) – each prayer linked to a brief passage of Scripture to aid reflection.

I do not claim to have created poetic masterpieces in these pages. That is not my aim. It is rather to articulate some of my own concerns in prayer in such a way that they may speak also for you. Within the five headings I explore many everyday emotions – joy, sorrow, hope, fear, faith, doubt – together with wider issues such as bereavement, the environment, injustice and exploitation. Above all, the emphasis is on responding to God, through word and deed, and asking his help to know, love and serve him better. I may not win you over to poetry, but if I help you to pray more meaningfully I will have succeeded in my goal.

NICK FAWCETT

PRAISE AND WORSHIP

1
Coming with awe

Come and see what God has done,
how awesome his works on our behalf!
Psalm 66:5

God of life, I come in worship,
lost in wonder, filled with awe.
At your feet I kneel in homage,
here to marvel and adore.
Words cannot express your greatness,
awesome is your majesty:
higher than the highest mountain,
deeper than the deepest sea.

God of love, I come rejoicing,
here to celebrate your grace.
Consecrate this sacred moment,
help me meet you face to face.
In the love of Christ enfold me,
by his touch make me anew:
cleanse, renew, restore, refashion
all I am and all I do.

God of light, I come in gladness,
soul on fire and heart ablaze,
reaching out in adoration,
singing hymns and songs of praise.
Take the hope that flames within me,
take the joy that burns so bright;
may my life reflect your glory,
finding favour in your sight.

2
The wonder of creation

The heavens proclaim the glory of God.
Psalm 19:1

The beauty of dew in the morning
and the chorus of birds in the trees,
the thrill of a new day dawning,
the hum of life on the breeze;
so much within creation
enthuses and uplifts.
O Lord, you bring elation
through all your many gifts.

Through the peace of twilight falling,
the sun setting low in the sky,
the sound of a blackbird calling,
the sparkling stars on high;
through these, O Lord, you bless us,
your power in each displayed.
Receive my praise and worship
for all that you have made.

3
A world of splendour

You are worthy, O Lord our God,
to receive glory and honour and power,
for all things were made by you,
their creation and existence down to your will.
Revelation 4:11

Lord, you created a world rich in splendour,
touched with a beauty no words can express,
able to move me to outbursts of wonder,
so much to savour and so much to bless.

Mountains and moorlands rise up to the heavens,
rivers and streams tumble down to the sea,
gifts that amaze in profusion surround me,
each a reflection of your majesty.

Promise of springtime and harvest of autumn,
cold winter mornings and warm summer days,
season by season brings cause for rejoicing,
reason to thank you and reason to praise.

Deep in the forest, remote in the desert,
down in the ocean or high in the air;
life in abundance is everywhere round me,
proof of your power and sign of your care.

Lord, you have given a world rich in splendour,
touched with a beauty that fills me with awe;
hear now my praises, I bring you my worship,
with all creation I kneel and adore.

4
God with us

I will be with you every day,
to the very end of time.
Matthew 28:20

For the knowledge day by day
you'll be with me, come what may;
for the fact my whole life through
you've been faithful, ever-true;
for the many ways you bless,
more than words can quite express;
living Lord, with heart ablaze,
full of joy, I bring you praise.

5

The God who loves us as we are

The Lord does not see as people see.
They look at appearances, but he sees into the heart.
1 Samuel 16:7b

You see me as no one else starts to,
the person concealed deep inside,
the weaknesses, faults and temptations,
the defects I'd much rather hide.
You see me laid bare of pretension,
the surface veneer stripped away,
the failings I cannot quite conquer
exposed to the cold light of day.
And yet you continue to love me,
your mercy and grace shining through;
despite all the times that I fail you,
you carry on making me new.
Such love is too awesome to credit,
like no other love that I know,
but though, Lord, I can't quite believe it,
you show me each day it is so.

6
God's awesome devotion

How precious, O God, is your unfailing love.
Psalm 36:7a

In the passionate care of a mother
and the heartfelt concern of a friend,
in the tender embrace of a lover,
in commitment that nothing can end,
I glimpse, gracious God, just a fraction
of the place I enjoy in your heart,
of your love shown so clearly in action
breaking down all that keeps us apart:
your sacrifice – suffering and dying –
to draw us once more to your side,
your mercy that never stops trying,
your purpose that won't be denied.
Such wonderful love leaves me reeling,
amazed it can ever be true.
Lord, grant me the same depth of feeling
in all of my dealings with you.

7
A love like none other

Whoever does not love knows nothing of God,
for God is love. God demonstrated his love like this:
he sent his only Son into the world
in order that we might live through him.
1 John 4:8, 9

For love so rich and special –
like nothing else on earth –
that found me, lost and hopeless,
and brought new life to birth;
that sees my many failings
yet loves me just the same,
and though it meets rejection
still seeks me out by name;
that knows my faith can waver,
enough at times to break,
yet gave itself completely,
faced anguish for my sake;
for love like this, so precious,
I give you, Lord, my praise,
my heart alight with wonder,
my spirit set ablaze.
Receive my grateful worship
and help me show, I pray,
a fraction of the ardour
you show to me each day.

8

For everything God has done and continues to do

To him, our only Saviour,
who is able to keep our feet from slipping,
and to present us faultless and brimming over with joy
into the glorious presence of God –
to him be glory and sovereignty,
dominion and authority, now and always.
Amen.
Jude: 24, 25

For the message I've believed,
all the mercy I've received,
heavy burdens you've relieved,
hear my praise.

For the life you've helped me start,
countless blessings you impart,
gift of joy within my heart,
hear my praise.

For the constant love you show,
priceless truth I've come to know,
living faith you've caused to grow,
hear my praise.

For your grace that makes me whole,
perfect peace within my soul,
precious prize you've made my goal,
hear my praise.

For the heavy loads you bear,
countless pointers that you care,
certain knowledge you are there,
hear my praise.

For the life you hold in store,
lived with you for evermore,
giving hope so strong, so sure,
hear my praise.

9
Joyful response

Worthy is the Lamb, sacrificed for us,
to receive power and riches,
wisdom and strength,
glory and blessing!
Revelation 5:12

Warm as the sun,
fresh as the breeze,
fair as a flower,
tall as the trees,
clear as the dew,
pure as the dove,
so unto me,
Lord, is your love.

Lovely as dawn,
welcome as light,
peaceful as dusk,
restful as night,
high as the clouds,
deep as the sea,
so is your love,
Lord, unto me.

Swift as a stream,
free as a bird,
firm as a rock,
sure as your word,

bright as the stars
shining above,
so unto me,
Lord, is your love.

Bursting with joy,
leaping with praise,
glowing with thanks,
heart set ablaze,
Lord, I would serve,
always be true –
such is my love,
Jesus, for you.

10
God's great goodness

We have redemption in him through his blood,
our sins forgiven through the riches of his grace
that he heaped upon us.
Ephesians 1:7, 8a

Gracious God, you give to me
more than I can ever need –
joy to last me all my days,
love that makes me blessed indeed.
Though I'm poor, you make me rich;
though I'm weak, in you I'm strong.
Lord, I lift my heart in praise,
lift my voice in joyful song.

Gracious God, you give to me
more than I could ever ask –
light to point the way ahead,
endless sun in which to bask,
life beyond my wildest dreams,
hope that will not ever die.
Lord, once more I sing your praise,
lift your holy name on high!

11
Heartfelt praise

I will acknowledge the Lord with all my heart.
I offer thanks in your name
for your unfailing love and constancy;
your name and your love are exalted
above everything.
Psalm 138:1a, 2b

O Lord, I want to praise you,
your holy name confess,
your mighty deeds acknowledge,
your awesome love express.
I want to give you worship,
to lift your name on high,
yet somehow words are lacking
however hard I try.

O Lord, I want to praise you,
through all I say and do,
to so live out the gospel
that all may know it's true.
I want to bring you glory,
to help your kingdom grow,
yet though I strive to serve you,
it rarely seems to show.

O Lord, I want to praise you,
to celebrate your love,
to thank you for the blessings
you pour down from above.

I want to bring you honour,
respond with all my heart,
yet sacrifice is costly –
I rarely even start.

O Lord, I want to praise you,
poor though my words may be;
although my faults are many
I come still, joyfully.
For though I often fail you
and know you but in part,
you look beneath the surface
and see what's in my heart.

12
Responding to God's grace

God demonstrated his love for us like this:
through Christ offering his life for us
even though our lives were steeped in wrongdoing.
Romans 5:8

Lord, I come to worship, not because I should,
not to claim I'm worthy, virtuous or good,
not because I'm special, different to the crowd,
having any merit, reason to be proud.
Rather, I come humbly, conscious of my need,
knowing I've been faithless, false in word and deed.
Day by day I stumble, miss the goals I seek;
though I mean to serve you, inwardly I'm weak.
Lord, I can't deceive you, hide what's deep inside,
yet you bid me welcome, arms extended wide.
Gratefully I worship, coming not in fear,
but responding gladly, thankful to be here.
I will try to follow, walk the Christian way,
not because I have to, but because I may.

13
An outpouring of praise

Despite not having seen him, you love him;
and although you do not yet see him,
you believe in him
and rejoice with an inexpressible and wonderful joy,
for you are obtaining the fruits of your faith,
the salvation of your souls.
1 Peter 1:8, 9

Lord, with a heart that leaps for sheer delight,
I bring the worship which is yours by right;
year after year you've blessed this life of mine,
turning what once was water into wine.

Lord, with a tongue that cries in joyful song,
gladly I praise you for your love so strong;
each day you bless me, always by my side;
come rain or sunshine you are there to guide.

Lord, with a mind that soars in grateful praise,
I will acclaim you, now and all my days;
you bring me hope, unbounded joy and love,
life in abundance streaming from above.

14
Celebrating God's
wonderful blessings

The Sovereign One has done wonderful things for me.
Honoured be his name!
Luke 1:49

You thrill and excite,
astound and amaze,
bring joy and delight
in so many ways.
Each day through your grace,
you cleanse and forgive
enfold and embrace,
equip me to live.
You nurture and lead,
renew and restore,
respond to my need
and do so much more.
For love so complete,
enriching my days,
I kneel at your feet,
and give, Lord, my praise.

15
For God's presence,
seen and unseen

He himself has categorically declared,
'I will never leave you or forsake you.'
Hebrews 13:5b

For the days when you feel near,
for the times when all is clear;
when your presence seems so real
that it colours all I feel –
for the blessing of such days,
Lord, accept my grateful praise.

For the times when you feel far,
when I wonder where you are;
when I call and call again,
but my prayers appear in vain –
when it seems you just don't care,
even then, Lord, you are there.

For the truth that day by day
you are present, come what may:
when I see you, when I don't,
when I trust you, when I won't –
for the peace these thoughts impart,
Lord, I come with thankful heart.

16
The unchanging God

I, the Lord, do not change.
Malachi 3:6a

So much in life, Lord, has shifted,
so much is different and strange;
everything somehow has drifted –
only your love does not change.

So much around me is fleeting,
here for a moment then gone;
Old Father Time brooks no cheating –
only your love carries on.

So much I loved, Lord, has vanished,
now just a memory or name;
into posterity banished –
only your love stays the same.

So much I think to be certain
proves in the end to be frail;
history brings down the curtain –
only your love will not fail.

17

Celebrating the God who meets us as Father, Son and Holy Spirit

The grace of the Lord Jesus Christ, the love of God,
and the fellowship of the Holy Spirit be with you all.
2 Corinthians 13:13

God of life, God of truth,
I rejoice that you are with me,
never distant or aloof.
Like a father, you are there,
reaching out your arms to hold me,
speaking words that show you care.

God of life, God of grace,
you have walked this earth before me,
giving truth a human face.
Knowing sorrow, knowing pain,
you were beaten, bruised and broken,
but in triumph rose again.

God of life, God of love –
felt as wind and tongues of fire
yet as gentle as a dove –
every moment, every hour,
you are working deep within me
through your sovereign selfless power.

God of life, God on high,
I can barely grasp your goodness,
language fails me when I try.
As a Father, through your Son,
by the Spirit you are with us,
somehow three, yet also one.

18
Celebrating God's gifts

If you who are flawed
know how to give good gifts to your children,
how much more will your heavenly Father
give good things to those who ask him!
Matthew 7:11

You are the giver of love,
holding my life in your hands,
filling my heart and feeding my soul,
granting your grace from above.

You are the giver of light,
shining on me and on all,
yearning to help and ready to guide,
bringing an end to the night.

You are the giver of joy,
aching to fill me with cheer,
making me glad and bringing delight,
bliss that no ill can destroy.

You are the giver of peace,
striving to make the world whole,
hungry to heal and thirsty to mend,
longing for hatred to cease.

You are the giver of all,
eager to bless me each day,
hands open wide, you freely impart
gifts to enrich and enthral.

19
Celebrating God's love

I will sing unceasingly of your unfailing love, O Lord;
I will declare your faithfulness to all generations.
Your constant love is unchanged
from the beginning of time,
and your faithfulness is as permanent as the heavens.
Psalm 89:1, 2

Like a bird soaring into flight,
like the moon glowing in the night,
like a flame, radiant with light,
so, O Lord, is your love in my sight.

Like a gift worthy of a king,
like a bud shooting in the spring,
like a bond signalled by a ring,
so each day is the love that you bring.

Like the dawn, fresh with morning dew,
like the sea, old but ever new,
like a dream, somehow coming true,
is the love that I find, Lord, in you.

Like a sign, pointing out the way,
like a field, sweet with summer hay,
like a stream, flowing come what may,
so, O Lord, is your love every day.

CONFESSION AND FORGIVENESS

20
Confessing our weakness

I do not understand why I act as I do.
For I end up doing the things I hate
rather than the things I want to do.
Romans 7:15

I've failed to love you, Father,
as much as you love me,
content to offer, rather,
a feeble travesty,
a going through the motions,
a playing of the part;
too often my devotions
not springing from the heart.
I truly mean to follow,
but other voices call;
discipleship proves hollow
as yet again I fall.
Commitment proves expensive,
temptations lead astray,
demands prove too extensive,
self-interest wins the day.
Lord, hear my supplications,
have mercy and forgive;
see past the limitations
that scar the love I give.
Remould, renew, refashion,
that I might learn your way,
responding with the passion
you show to me each day.

21

Acknowledging our failure
to live up to our intentions

It almost seems to be a law
that whenever I intend to do good,
evil is there as well,
for while inwardly I delight in God's law,
I see a different law in my body
battling with the law of my mind,
enslaving me to the law of sin
that dwells in my members.
Romans 7:21-23

Lord of my life, have mercy I pray,
I've failed you again, abandoned your way.
Your love I've betrayed, your truth I've denied,
intending to serve, I've strayed from your side.
Deal kindly I ask, from sin set me free;
see not what I am, but all I would be.
Redeem and restore, forgive and renew.
Come, Lord, in your grace, and help me stay true.

22
A plea for forgiveness

Forgive me, Lord,
in accordance with your unfailing love;
through your overflowing grace
erase any trace of my sins from the record.
For I'm all too aware of them,
constantly haunted by the error of my ways.
Psalm 51:1, 3

Lord, I know that I have failed you,
false and foolish in so much,
loath to listen to your guidance,
slow to recognise your touch.
Though I keep you at a distance,
by my side, Lord, still remain;
cleanse my heart, renew my spirit,
give me grace to start again.

Lord, I know that I have failed you
through the things I do and say;
though I claim to care for others
I have thrust their needs away.
Too concerned with my own comfort,
I have added to their pain;
teach me to put faith in action,
give me grace to start again.

Lord, I know that I have failed you,
full of doubt when life's been hard;
suffering has sapped my vision,
sorrow left my spirit scarred.

Faced by bitter disappointment
faith has buckled under strain;
help me know your hand upon me,
give me grace to start again.

Lord, I know that I have failed you,
too familiar with your word,
even though you've spoken clearly
all too often I've not heard.
Closed to truths which stretch horizons
or which go against the grain –
help me, Lord, to stop and listen,
give me grace to start again.

Lord, I know that I have failed you,
life too fraught to stop and stare;
focused too much on the present –
what to eat or drink or wear.
Teach me first to seek your kingdom;
in my heart for ever reign;
send me out, restored, forgiven,
give me grace to start again.

23
Seeking renewal

If we claim to have no sin, we are fooling ourselves
and the truth has no place in us.
If we confess our sins, he is just,
and we can rely on him to forgive our sins
and cleanse us from all evil.
1 John 1:8, 9

Lord, forgive me, I am weak,
seldom do the things I seek,
rarely serve you as I should –
wrong prevails instead of good.
By your grace come make me whole --
mind and body, heart and soul.
Where I'm false help me be true;
wash me clean and make me new.

24
Acknowledging our need to grow in faith

Just as the heavens are beyond the earth,
so are my ways beyond your ways,
and my thoughts outside your thoughts.
Isaiah 55:9

For thinking I can ever know
the way you have things planned,
forgetting that I need to grow
if I would understand;
for feeling you can be contained
by my poor reach of mind,
assuming truth can be explained
or rigidly defined;
for all the ways my faith is flawed
and understanding skewed,
I ask your pardon, gracious Lord,
and beg to be renewed.

25
Acknowledging our failure
to translate faith into action

I tell you the truth, whenever you offered service
to the least of individuals, you offered it also to me.
Matthew 25:40

I'm not an angel, nowhere near,
I often go astray,
but though my faults are all too clear,
I try, Lord, to obey.
Avoid what's evil, strive for good,
that's been my daily aim –
to live the sort of life I should
in keeping with your name.
But now I see that this alone
can never fully do;
instead it's how much love I've shown
that matters most to you –
if, when I saw a friend in need,
a person in despair,
I paid their plight sufficient heed,
enough to show I care.
My times of worship, hymns and prayers
each have their part to play,
but only if my life declares
the truth of what I say;
if what I am and what I do
stays faithful to your call,
in showing love not just to you
but equally to all.

26
Confessing the shallowness of our commitment

Little children, let us love,
not in word or empty promise,
but in deed and reality.
1 John 3:18

Lord, I sometimes come to worship
thinking you will be impressed
by some outward show of homage –
putting on my Sunday best –
but you say the clothes don't matter,
nor the public face I wear,
but the person underneath them,
what lies hidden under there.

I may wear a friendly smile,
talk of helping those in need,
but the words I use so freely
are not always matched by deed.
Though I read the Bible daily,
go to church, excel in prayer,
none of this is worth a farthing
if I fail to show I care.

Anyone can preach forgiveness,
tell the world it's wrong to judge;
anyone can talk of loving,
yet still bear a secret grudge;

anyone can speak of treasure
far exceeding worldly wealth;
but such sentiments ring hollow
if I only think of self.

Lord, forgive me that so often
I put on an outer show,
hiding from myself and others
what I'd rather no one know.
Help me to be truly honest,
see where words are but a sham.
May the faith I claim to follow
show itself in who I am.

27
Acknowledging the folly of pride

Pride goes before an undoing,
and an arrogant spirit before a fall.
It is better to take a seat humbly among the poor
than to divide the spoil with the proud.
Proverbs 16:18, 19

For the foolishness of pride
and the hurt to which it leads;
for the value I've denied
to my neighbours' words and deeds;
for the failings I condemn,
and the flaws I'm swift to see,
all those faults I find with them
yet can never spot in me;
for dismissing every view
running counter to my own,
overlooking people's gifts,
having time for mine alone,
grant your pardon, God, I pray;
call me back, before I fall;
help me take the Saviour's way
and respect the worth of all.

28

Recognising our share
in the abuse of creation

The earth is the Lord's and everything in it,
the world and all those who live in it.
In his hand are the innermost parts of the earth,
and the mountain peaks belong to him.
The sea is his, for he made it,
and his hands shaped the dry land.
Psalm 24:1; 95:4

You've given a world, Lord, of untold delight,
that moves me to worship and praise;
that speaks of your glory by day and by night –
so much there to thrill and amaze.
The peak of a mountain, the shade of a tree,
the colour and scent of a flower,
the peace of a river or wrath of the sea –
each gives me a glimpse of your power.
The laughter of children, the crunching of leaves,
or delicate song of a bird,
the hum of a city, the whispering breeze –
in so much your voice can be heard.
Forgive me, I pray, the indictment I share
for failing to steward this Earth,
neglecting to give it due honour or care,
and losing a sense of its worth.
I squander resources, betraying your trust,
yet somehow I don't seem to learn.
Lord, help me to treasure this world as I must –
that others might share it in turn.

29

Acknowledging our failure
to love God
as fully as we should

You shall love the Lord your God
with all your heart, all your soul, and all your mind.
This is the first and greatest commandment.
Matthew 22:37, 38

I offered songs of worship,
knelt down to you in prayer.
I sought your will and guidance,
and read your word with care.
I went to church each Sunday
and pledged to walk your way,
resolved to serve you better,
determined to obey.
To everyone around me,
I must have looked the part –
yet one thing, Lord, was lacking:
true worship from the heart.

30
Celebrating God's
<u>undeserved mercy</u>

We see love most completely in this:
not in us having loved God
but in he loving us so much that he sent his Son
to put right our relationship with him.
God is love; all those who live in love
live also in God, and he in them.
1 John 4:10, 16b

I have no claim on your love at all,
no grounds to seek clemency;
I mean to serve, but repeatedly fall,
my faithlessness plain to see.
The vows I've made, commitment professed,
all seem to have been in vain,
as faults and flaws so often confessed
return to haunt me again.
You see the worst, all my ugliness,
all that poisons deep inside,
but still you love, always eager to bless,
refusing to be denied.
No words, O Lord, can begin to say
how much I will always owe;
no sacrifice even start to repay
the mercy and grace you show.
I give you thanks, bring my all to you,
amazed that such love can be –
so rich and full, so constant and true,
so priceless and yet so free.

31
Celebrating God's
unfailing grace

I have come that you might have life,
and have it abundantly.
John 10:10b

Have I failed to live as I ought to,
to serve you as I should?
Have I flouted your will and denied you,
and turned my back on good?
Am I thoughtless, selfish and greedy,
concerned with self alone,
expecting the hungry and needy
to get by on their own?
The answer, Lord, hardly needs saying –
all this is true and more:
my life far too often displaying
mistakes I've made before.
But though such betrayals may grieve you,
they cause you hurt far less
than how often I undervalue
the ways you long to bless.
You offer me life overflowing,
more blessed than words can say.
Lord, help me to thank you by showing
how much it means, each day.

THANKSGIVING

32

For what we so often take for granted

Be still, and know that I am God.
Psalm 46:10a

Lord, today your voice is calling,
lifting thoughts to things above;
life is wonderful, enthralling,
touched by your unfailing love.
Suddenly I see the beauty
often hidden from my gaze,
so I come not out of duty,
but with glad and grateful praise.

Lord, I sometimes fail to value
all your blessings as I should;
slow to make due time to thank you,
blind to so much that is good.
Days are lived in such a hurry
there's no time to stop and stare;
joy is crushed by weight of worry,
happiness obscured by care.

Lord, today I come rejoicing,
vowed to waste your gifts no more;
bringing praise and gladly voicing
what I should have voiced before.
Pouring out my adulation,
scarcely knowing where to start,
with a song of exultation,
Lord, I thank you from the heart.

33
For the cycle of the seasons

For as long as this world continues,
seedtime and harvest, warm days and cold,
summer and winter, day and night,
will never fail.
Genesis 8:22

For summer and autumn, winter and spring,
the breathtaking beauty these faithfully bring –
lengthening days calling new life to birth,
delicate blooms bursting fresh from the earth;
sunshine and showers, heat mist and haze,
fragrance and colour to thrill and amaze;
ripening fruit, golden sheaves in the field,
harvest thanksgiving at Earth's gracious yield;
holly and ivy, a nip in the air,
frost-covered branches, their glory laid bare –
Lord, for this cycle so special and true,
life always changing yet ever made new,
hear now my worship, and help me, I pray,
gladly to honour creation each day.

34
For the promise of new life

Nothing that you sow can spring to life
unless it dies first.
For whatever you plant is transitory,
but what rises from this will never die.
1 Corinthians 15:36b, 42b

Lord, autumn leaves are falling,
the trees will soon be bare;
a multitude of endings
surround me everywhere.
So much that bloomed so brightly
now seems a world away,
its glory but a memory,
supplanted by decay.
Yet, hidden in the darkness,
beneath the silent earth,
already shoots are forming –
a promise of new birth.
And, softly, you are saying,
to those with ears to hear,
though death for now brings sorrow,
keep hope and do not fear.
Yes, life may seem extinguished,
but days to come will bring
beginnings after endings,
in place of winter, spring.

35
For blessings
we all too often overlook

I have learned to be content in everything,
no matter what life might bring.
Philippians 4:11b

When I fret about the things life might have brought,
when I fail to count my blessings as I ought,
when I moan about my lot,
pine for what I haven't got,
scarcely give what I've received a second thought,
teach me, Lord, to look again, that I may see
all the special gifts you grant so lavishly –
so much beauty everywhere,
so much speaking of your care,
boundless blessing, priceless treasure, mine for free.
Help me prove I've understood that truth, I pray
in a way that words alone just can't convey:
may the happiness you give
show itself in how I live –
in a life that shines with thanks and praise each day.

36
For God's constant help

Come what may, we can confidently say,
'The Lord is my helper, I will not be afraid.
What can anyone do to me?'
Hebrews 13:6

Lord, you don't promise us comfort and wealth,
freedom from sickness, immaculate health:
faith brings no pledge of exemption from pain,
troubles oppress us again and again;
tragedies cause us to grieve and despair,
sometimes their burden too painful to bear;
visions are shattered and hopes turned to dust,
prayer seems in vain, though we try still to trust.
Yet, though such trials turn out to be true,
still I believe you will help me get through –
there by my side when I can't carry on,
offering strength when all other has gone.
Even in sorrow you somehow bring joy,
peace that no trials can ever destroy.
Light in the darkness continues to shine,
turning the water of life into wine.

37

For God's unfailing love

The Lord is the strength of his people,
a safe refuge for his anointed.
Psalm 28:8

I've talked of trusting come what may,
of walking where you lead;
I've pledged to follow day by day,
to serve in word and deed;
I've claimed to love you, heart and soul,
enough to give my all –
yet though such faith has been my goal
repeatedly I fall.

Lord, thankfully the love *you* show
is of a different kind –
a love that will not let me go
no matter what you find.
However much I fail to be
the person I intend,
in you I find true constancy,
one faithful to the end.

38
For love we cannot start to repay

God loved the world so much
that he offered his only Son,
in order that all those who believe in him,
instead of dying, will enjoy eternal life.
John 3:16

Jesus, you died for me,
suffered to set me free,
gave all so willingly.

Jesus, in love you came,
bore all my sin and shame,
faultless, you took the blame.

Jesus, you've brought me light,
put dark despair to flight,
healed me and set me right.

Jesus, you've made me new,
touched all I say and do.
Can love like this be true!

Jesus, what can I say?
I can't such love repay,
yet I must find some way.

Jesus, my Lord and King,
my love to you I bring,
my life, my everything.

39
For God's strength and protection

God is our sanctuary and protection,
a constant help in times of peril.
So we will fear nothing,
even if this world should be turned upside down
and the mountains crumble into the depths of the ocean –
even if the waters of the sea thunder and churn
and the mountains quiver amid the turmoil.
Psalm 46:1-3

I do not know what life may hold,
if good or ill I'll see,
what twists and turns may yet unfold,
what trials yet might be.
I cannot say if light will shine
or darkness fall once more,
what destiny might still be mine,
what future lies in store.
But even if the way is tough
and storms begin to blow,
the gales prove strong, the water rough,
one thing, Lord, still I know:
that you'll be there, supporting me,
a faithful, loving guide –
a constant help who will not fail
to strengthen and provide.
I have no need to ask for more
nor any cause to fear:
whatever life may hold for me
I know that you'll be near.

40
For the knowledge that God is always by our side

I will ask the Father, and he will give you
another comforter to be with you for ever.
I will not abandon you to your fate; I will come to you.
John 14:16, 18

When I'm feeling low,
nowhere left to go,
always, Lord, you show
you are there, every step that I go.

When I'm in despair,
spirit crushed by care,
life too hard to bear,
you are there – every step, everywhere.

When my dreams have died,
hopes have been denied,
nowhere left to hide,
still you're there, every step by my side.

When I need a friend
aching wounds to tend,
broken heart to mend,
you are there, every step to the end.

Every single day,
by my side you stay,
with me, come what may,
always there, every step of the way.

41
For the knowledge
that God's love will never fail

The Lord is my rock, fortress and deliverer.
He is my rock, the one in whom I take refuge,
my shield and source of salvation,
a stronghold, refuge and saviour.
2 Samuel 22:2, 3a

I've tasted pain and sadness,
the bitterness of tears,
yet also known such gladness,
such joy across the years;
so much that's brought me pleasure,
more blessed than words can say,
experiences to treasure,
enchantment day by day.
Yes, darker times have faced me,
some difficult to meet,
but always you've embraced me
and set me on my feet.
Lord, whether celebration
will mark the days ahead,
or bitter desolation
will be my lot instead,
of one thing I am certain –
experience tells me so –
your love will never fail me
or ever let me go.

42

For God's constant presence

I trust in you, O Lord; I say, 'You are my God.'
My times are in your hand.
Psalm 31:14, 15a

Every hour, every minute,
every day I give to you,
for I know you're with me in it,
reaching out to bless anew.
Take the present and tomorrow,
take my laughter and my tears;
whether I know joy or sorrow,
buoyant hopes or nagging fears.
All I'm facing, all I'm feeling,
Lord, I place into your hands,
for in you is inner healing –
one who cares and understands.
Though I'm weak and hesitating,
you are there to help and guide.
Always, Lord, I find you waiting,
ever-present by my side.

43

For the God who will not fail us

The enduring love of the Lord never fades,
his mercies can never be exhausted; each morning
they are made new, such is his great faithfulness.
'The Lord is all I need,' declares my soul,
'and so I will trust in him.'
Lamentations 3:22-24

Lord, you have blessed me and filled me with joy,
granting me life that no ill can destroy.
Day after day brings new reason to praise,
blessings to thrill and delights to amaze.
Guidance, forgiveness, renewal and grace,
strength and support in whatever I face,
peace beyond words, constant help from above –
so much each moment affirms your great love.
Morning by morning new mercies I see,
gifts beyond number and all of them free.
How can I thank you, Lord? Where can I start?
Hear now my worship – it comes from the heart.

44
For faith in things unseen

What we can see is transient – here today and gone
tomorrow. Eternal things are hidden from our sight.
2 Corinthians 4:18

I do not know what heaven is,
the where or when or how;
if it's a kingdom yet to come
or all around us now.
I cannot claim to understand
the complex ins and outs –
in fact, along with faith I have
a healthy share of doubts.
So am I whistling in the dark,
just clutching hold of straws,
content to cling to anything
that soothes and reassures?
Is dread of facing up to truth
the root of my belief;
this hope of mine some cosy way
of coping with my grief?
It's true I'll never prove that life
continues after death,
to claim that it is otherwise
is just a waste of breath.
That one day we will rise again,
not simply turn to dust,
cannot be shown by argument,
but has to rest on trust.
Our faith in what God holds in store
goes deeper than the mind,

not solely based on reasoning
but of another kind:
its source the one who died, yet lives
and walks with us each day,
whose gracious love encircles all
each step along the way.
In him I find a certainty
on which I can depend,
for love like this, so full, so free,
can surely never end.

45

For release of a loved one from pain and suffering

The souls of the faithful are in God's hands,
pain no longer able to touch them.
Those who know no better believe them to have died,
and consider death to be a tragedy,
their parting to have robbed them of life,
but they are at peace. The faithful live for evermore
and the sovereign God will take care of them.
Wisdom of Solomon 3:1-3

I saw my loved one suffer,
each moment touched with pain,
the body slowly failing,
too weak to take the strain.
I knew each day brought testing,
more cruel than words can tell,
until life, once so special,
became a living hell:
the only thing that mattered,
at last to be at peace;
the only goal to strive for,
to somehow find release;
no reason still to struggle
or cause to fear the end;
an enemy no longer,
death beckoned as a friend.
At last the pain is over –
it falls to me instead –
Lord, may that knowledge help me
to face the days ahead.

46

For confidence in God, come what may

Even though I walk through the darkest of valleys,
I fear no evil, for you are with me,
your rod and staff a constant source of comfort.
Psalm 23:4

Though this day brings good or bad,
makes me happy, leaves me sad,
leads to smiles, ends in tears,
answers hopes or bears out fears;
whether I prove weak or strong,
do things right or get them wrong;
gracious Lord, through good or ill,
thank you that you're with me still.

47
For love we can depend on

You keep in perfect peace those whose minds are
focused on you, because in you they find their trust.
Isaiah 26:3

No more worry, you are here,
bringing peace instead of fear,
reaching out in tender care,
sharing burdens, hard to bear.
From the old you bring the new,
giving strength to see me through.
Lord, on you I can depend,
for your love will never end.

48
For God's faithful guidance

I will not fail or forsake you.
Joshua 1:5b

Day after day, Lord you are there,
speaking your word, hearing my prayer,
glad to respond, eager to bless,
happy to help, pleased to say yes.

Day after day, Lord you are near,
granting your peace, banishing fear,
slow to rebuke, swift to inspire,
filling with joy, lighting a fire.

Week after week, Lord you provide,
hungry to teach, ready to guide,
proving your love, showing concern,
helping me grow, helping me learn.

Month after month, Lord you stay true,
giving me strength, seeing me through,
lighting my path, leading the way,
seeking me out if should stray.

Year after year, Lord you forgive,
cleansing my faults, helping me live.
Love fills my heart, floods through my soul,
healing my wounds, making me whole.

49
For peace that passes <u>understanding</u>

I give you my peace – that's the legacy I leave you,
unlike anything the world can give.
So, then, do not let your heart be anxious or afraid.
John 14:27

Lord, you have touched my life,
brought an end to inner strife,
in confusion, made me still,
resting in your perfect will.

Lord, you have touched my mind,
helped me quietness to find,
caused the storms within to cease,
set my thoughts at perfect peace.

Lord, you have touched my heart,
brought relief in every part,
taught me how to stop and stare,
and to glimpse you everywhere.

Lord, you have touched my soul,
worked within to make me whole.
All is calm, you've brought me rest.
Truly I am richly blessed!

50

For the richness
of God's blessings

Blessed be the God and Father
of our Lord Jesus Christ,
who has bestowed on us in Christ
every spiritual blessing in the heavenly realms.
Ephesians 1:3

Wonderful, great is your love for me,
richer than words can ever say,
day after day new mercies I see,
blessings too special to repay.
How can I show what you mean to me?
Any response seems far too small.
What fitting thanks could there ever be?
Nothing can hope to say it all.
Yet I would show that my faith is real,
prove that my love for you is true.
Take what I say, what I think and feel;
all that I am, I bring to you.

51
For God's gift of laughter

A merry heart makes for a cheerful countenance,
but a morose disposition crushes the spirit.
Every day in life is wretched for the downtrodden,
yet those with a cheerful heart feast continually.
Proverbs 15:13, 15

Think of a world without any laughter,
think of a life without any wit;
think of a day without any humour,
think of a sermon without any quips.
I thank you, Lord, for laughter, wit and humour;
I thank you, Lord, and praise your holy name.

Think of a world without any smiling,
think of a party without any fun;
think of a joke without any punchline,
think of a language without rhyme or pun.
I thank you, Lord, for smiling, fun and punchlines;
I thank you, Lord, and praise your holy name.

Think of a world without any comedy,
think of a circus without any clowns;
think of a court without any jester,
think of a home without merry sounds.
I thank you, Lord, for comics, clowns and jesters;
I thank you, Lord, and praise your holy name.

Think of a world where all must be serious,
think of a church were everyone's grim;
think of a life where laughter is frowned upon,

think of a faith where humour is sin.
I thank you, Lord, for all we have to cheer us;
I thank you, Lord, and praise your holy name.

(*adapted from a hymn by Doreen Newport*)

52

For everything a loved one meant to us

You have transformed my grief into celebration,
clothing me with gladness rather than funeral attire,
so that instead of keeping quiet,
my soul sings out in praise.
Lord God, I would offer you heartfelt thanks,
now and always.
Psalm 30:11, 12

In the sorrow that I'm feeling
as I try to take things in;
though my broken heart is reeling,
and my mind is in a spin;
call to mind, Lord, all the pleasure
that I've shared across the years –
moments I will always treasure
with a smile as well as tears:
hands that nurtured and provided,
bandaged wounds and helped me grow;
words that comforted and guided,
teaching much of what I know;
times of happiness and laughter,
deeds that spoke of love and care,
days that I'll recall long after –
such a privilege to share.
Lord, although a weight of sadness
leaves me grieving and distressed,
deep within there's also gladness
for I've been so richly blessed.

53
For one we've loved and lost

He has sent me to comfort those who grieve,
to adorn them with garlands instead of ashes,
oil instead of mourner's tears,
a garment of praise instead of a heavy heart.
Isaiah 61:1b, 3a

I've lost one whom I loved, Lord,
more precious than can be,
who brought life joy and meaning,
and meant the world to me.
Each day I yearn for comfort,
yet cannot find relief –
the smile I wear in public,
a mask to hide my grief –
for all we shared is over,
its joy beyond recall;
a cloud obscures my vision
and overshadows all.
And yet, in scattered moments,
I glimpse another side –
although for now we're parted,
not everything has died:
the empathy between us,
the love that freely flowed,
the happiness and laughter,
the time and care bestowed,
all these have helped to bring me
to where I am today,
each one a priceless treasure
that death can't pluck away.

So when I'm feeling wretched,
dejected and bereft,
Lord, help me to remember
how much there still is left;
to recognise more fully
the blessings I've enjoyed:
their legacy continues
and will not be destroyed.

54
For hope beyond the grave

With the Lord's authority, I tell you this:
those of us who are alive, left waiting for his coming,
will not be given preference over those who have died.
Rather, those of us left alive
will mysteriously be caught up with them
into the heavens to meet him,
to be by his side for ever.
1 Thessalonians 4:15, 17

The time had come, a time to die –
with heavy heart I said goodbye.
The world felt bleak, my mind was numb,
for what I feared to see had come.
Someone so dear was dead and gone,
yet, Lord, through you, life carries on –
I don't know how, I don't when,
but, by your grace, we'll meet again.

55

For comfort in bereavement

The everlasting God is your eternal home;
his loving arms will support you for ever.
Deuteronomy 33:27

There's so much I wanted to say, Lord,
so much I wanted to do,
all kinds of hopes left unrealised,
dreams that I'll never see through:
news I would once have related,
deeds showing how much I cared,
love I intended to speak of –
all can no longer be shared.
Help me to face my emotions,
deal with the sorrow I feel,
cope with the pain of remembering,
such that, in time, these might heal.
Teach me to look back with gladness,
happy in spite of the tears,
grateful for wonderful memories,
joy spanning so many years.
So may I find consolation
when I feel lost and alone,
able to grieve with a smile,
thankful for all I have known.

56
For honest memories
of a loved one

Come what may, love makes allowances, keeps faith,
sees the best, continues undiminished.
It cannot be extinguished.
1 Corinthians 13:7, 8a

Lord, help me to remember
the person that I knew,
not some idealised portrait
no longer ringing true.
Remind me of each aspect,
the special and mundane,
the failings and the virtues,
the beautiful and plain,
the triumphs and the failures,
the happy and the sad,
the folly and the wisdom,
the good times and the bad,
the moments of contentment
and days of dark despair,
the words that spoke of anger
and deeds that spoke of care,
the laughter and the sorrow,
the pleasure and the pain,
the hopes that found fulfilment,
the dreams that proved in vain.
Not every trait was perfect,
nor every feature good,
not everything between us

worked out quite as it should,
but all these points together
combined in such a way
to craft one far more precious
than words can ever say –
a person whom I value
for everything they've been,
and one I'll go on loving
for what they'll always mean.

PETITION

57

For hope in times of confusion

I am convinced that nothing will ever be able
to separate us from Christ's love.
Neither death nor life, neither angels nor demons,
neither the present nor the future,
neither any powers, height or depth,
nor indeed anything else in all creation,
will ever be able to separate us from the love of God
that is ours in Christ Jesus our Lord.
Romans 8:38, 39

Though much in life bemuses
or flatters to deceive;
though what I face confuses,
denies what I believe;
though confidence is shattered
when evil wins the day,
and all my hopes seem battered,
my troubles here to stay;
though fortune leaves me shaken,
destroying every dream;
new faith, Lord, reawaken
that things aren't what they seem.
Assure me you are turning
the darkness into light,
that grace will keep on burning,
however deep the night.
Revive, refresh, restore me
when trust and vision pall –
renew the faith that surely
your love will conquer all.

58

For the assurance of God's presence in times of adversity

I am the Lord your God, who takes hold of your right
hand and says to you, 'Never fear: I will help you.' I,
the Lord, have called you in my goodness; I will take
hold of your hand.
Isaiah 41:13; 42:6

Though days are touched with sadness
and all appears in vain;
though every waking moment
my faith feels under strain;
though burdens weigh upon me
that seem too hard to bear;
Lord, speak your word of promise,
remind me you are there.

Though trusted friends forsake me
and I feel left alone;
though those I thought most loyal
have taken wings and flown;
though dreams lie bruised and broken
and no one sheds a tear;
Lord, speak your word of promise,
remind me you are here.

Though life is dark with shadows,
its lustre long since gone;
though winter's chill encroaches
where summer sun once shone;

though days that seemed to sparkle
are tarnished now with care;
Lord, speak your word of promise,
remind me you are there.

Though everything I hoped for
lies trampled in the dust;
though there seems nothing solid
in which to put my trust;
though worry holds me captive –
a slave to every fear;
Lord, speak your word of promise,
remind me you are here.

59
For light in our darkness

I call to you, O Lord my rock:
do not refuse to listen, for if you keep silent
I shall be like those who go down into the depths.
Hear my entreaty as I beg you for help,
and as I lift up my hands towards your dwelling place.
Psalm 28:1, 2

Living Lord, I cry to you,
in your mercy, hear my prayer:
come and show how much you care.

Loving Lord, I call to you,
in your goodness, hear my cry:
lift my broken spirit high.

In my darkness, bring your light,
grant your sunshine after night,
put my tears and fears to flight.

Though I seek and do not find,
still I call your love to mind,
ever gracious, ever kind.

Show me, Lord, your faithfulness,
sovereign in your holiness,
swift to save and sure to bless.

Living Lord, I cry to you,
knowing you make all things new:
take my hand and lead me through.

60
For peace in the storms of life

Take my yoke on you and learn from me,
for I am tender and lowly in heart
and you will find rest for your souls –
for my yoke is easy, and my burden is light.
Matthew 11:29, 30

Lord, I lift my hands to you in prayer,
mind in turmoil, overwhelmed by care.

'Come,' you say, 'and find rest for your soul.
Trust in me, and love will make you whole.'

Lord, I come, the storm within is stilled,
peace flows through me, your word has been fulfilled.

61
For help in a time of need

Save me, O God,
for the waters have come up to my neck.
Psalm 69:1

Help me, Lord, reach out to save;
hold me tight, or I am lost;
storms are breaking, wave on wave,
into turmoil life is tossed.
Come, I beg you, hear my call,
for I'm sinking like a stone;
faith is feeble, far too small –
I can't face this on my own.
You may tell me not to fear,
say that I should always hope,
but I cannot see you near –
how then am I meant to cope?
Wait! What's this? The tide is turning.
Once again, Lord, I was wrong.
Bit by bit, I'm slowly learning
when I'm weak then you are strong!

62
For hope
despite the way things seem

Cast all your worries on to him,
for he cares about you.
1 Peter 5:7

When I'm feeling crushed by care,
heavy burdens hard to bear;
when my heart, oppressed by grief,
looks in vain to find relief;
when I find it hard to trust,
hopes and dreams reduced to dust;
teach me, Lord, that you are near,
never mind how things appear,
reaching out to see me through,
ever-faithful, ever-true.

63
For God's saving help

Why am I disheartened and troubled in spirit?
I will put my hope afresh in you, O God,
for whatever happens I will praise you again,
my help and my God.
Psalm 42:5, 6a

Are you listening? Are you here?
Come and save me. Lord, draw near.
Day by day I'm losing hope,
fearful that I may not cope.
Trust is weak and faith is frail,
stretched until it starts to fail.
Yet I've felt this way before
and, despite it, you proved sure,
bringing joy instead of tears,
inner peace in place of fears.
Though I'm weak, Lord, *you* are strong,
there to help my whole life long.

64
For help in dealing with infirmity or poor health

We are not discouraged,
for even though we seem outwardly debilitated,
inwardly we are being renewed every day.
The inconsequential affliction we endure now
is preparing for us an eternal weight of glory
beyond measure.
2 Corinthians 4:16, 17

When days are filled with struggle
and nights are racked by pain,
when faculties are failing
and health is on the wane,
when living seems an effort,
past vigour long since gone,
and darkness starts encroaching
where once the sun had shone,
Lord, teach me you'll be with me,
to comfort and console –
that, though time wastes the body,
it cannot touch the soul.

When youth seems but a memory
and limbs are stiff and sore,
when daily I'm reminded
of things I'll do no more,
when inwardly I'm willing
but outwardly I'm weak,
and succour proves elusive,

no matter how I seek,
Lord, teach me you'll be with me,
to cherish and to mend –
that though this life is passing,
the grave is not the end.

When treasures start to tarnish,
as all things surely must,
when childhood dreams have faded
and hopes lie in the dust,
when life no longer sparkles
quite as it used to shine
and nothing can recapture
the joys that once were mine,
Lord, teach me you'll be with me,
to strengthen and sustain –
that, though the night is falling,
your light will shine again.

65

For help in understanding God's kingdom and bringing it closer

Blessed are those who hunger and thirst
for righteousness, for they will be satisfied.
Learn to seek the kingdom and righteousness of God
before all else, and you will be given everything else
you need in addition.
Matthew 5:6; 6:33

Jesus, the bread of life, I come to you;
empty, I would be fed – meet me anew.
Teach me to hunger after righteousness.
Reach out in love, I pray, to guide and bless.

Jesus, the poured-out wine, I come in awe;
thirsty, I long to drink – quench and restore.
Teach me to seek your kingdom and your will.
Reach out in love, I pray, my life to fill.

Jesus, the crucified, I come with shame;
greedy, I've served myself – made that my aim.
Teach me to worship now through word and deed.
Reach out in love, I pray, to all in need.

Jesus, the King of kings, I come to serve;
freely to honour you as you deserve.
Teach me to share the grace you daily show.
Reach out in love, I pray, and bid me go.

66
For strength to resist temptation

He is able now to offer help to all facing temptation,
since he was tempted likewise
and suffered for our sakes.
Hebrews 2:18

Lord, it isn't always easy,
to stay faithful to your call,
for, despite my best intentions,
there's so much that makes me fall.
Though the spirit may be willing,
all too often flesh is weak;
though I talk about your kingdom,
it's *this* world's rewards I seek.

Help me learn from your example,
all the trials you endured
as you wrestled in the desert
until victory was assured.
Teach me that you faced temptation
yet stayed faithful to the last,
putting thoughts of self behind you,
through all testing holding fast.

Save me, Lord, from ever thinking
there was no real choice to make;
that the journey set before you
was a simple one to take.
You were human, just as I am,
loving life and fearing pain,
but you took the path of suffering
rather than the way of gain.

When your body groaned with hunger
how you must have longed for bread,
and, compared to death, how lovely
living must have seemed instead.
Which of us in your shoes would have
carried on without some sign
that the sacrifice was worth it –
all a part of God's design?

Lord, you know it isn't easy
to stay faithful to your call,
for you faced the same temptations
which are common to us all.
May that knowledge give me courage
to resist what leads astray,
certain you will walk beside me
every step along my way.

67
For help to follow more faithfully

Fashion a new and unblemished heart
within me, O God;
imbue me with a true and faithful spirit.
Psalm 51:10

Where are the vows of long ago,
the promises I made,
the faith and trust I used to show,
the vision I displayed?
Where is the eagerness I knew
to follow day by day;
though others fail, to still stay true
and serve you come what may?
Where is the life I swore to lead,
the love I aimed to share,
the gentle word and thoughtful deed
that showed how much I care?
Lord, for all my lofty dreams
I've fallen so far short –
to walk the way of Christ, it seems,
is harder than I thought.
Make up in me the strength I lack
to stay true to your call,
for I would offer something back
to you who gave your all.

68
For faith in moments of doubt

Why, Lord, are you so distant?
Why do you conceal yourself in times of difficulty?
Psalm 10:1

What is the truth I'm seeking?
What do I hope to find?
Is it your voice that's speaking
or just some trick of the mind?
Why don't you hear my crying?
Why don't you answer prayer?
Why is the child dying?
Why don't you seem to care?
So much in life bemuses,
turning my faith to doubt;
so much obscures and confuses –
Lord, I can't work it out.
How can we call you caring,
faced by such sorrow and pain?
Is there not cause for despairing
when all our hopes seem in vain?
Lord, have you any suggestions?
Can all these riddles make sense?
I cannot stifle my questions,
cannot indulge in pretence.
Where rival answers are warring,
where I just don't understand,
teach me to keep on exploring,
striving to make out your hand.
Help me to search sincerely,
baring my soul to you;
even though *I* can't see clearly,
help me to trust that *you* do.

69
For answers to questions of faith

Lord, I believe; conquer my unbelief.
Mark 9:24

Lord, there are times when I need to ask, 'Why?' –
times when appearances give faith the lie.
Innocents suffer and evil holds sway.
Grant me some answers, Lord, teach me your way.

Lord, there are times when I need to ask, 'Where?' –
times when it seems that you simply don't care.
Though I call out, you seem distant, aloof.
Show me you're present, Lord, grant me some proof.

Lord, there are times when I need to ask, 'What?' –
times when your hand isn't easy to spot.
What is life's purpose and what of me here?
In my confusion, Lord, make your will clear.

Lord, there are times when I need to ask, 'How?' –
times when your promises clash with life now.
Wrestling with doubt I ask, 'How can this be?'
Give me some insight, Lord, help me to see.

Lord, there are times when the questions run fast –
times when I fear that my faith might not last.
Hear me, support me, and help me get through.
Lead me through darkness till light shines anew.

70
For help in making sense of loss

There is a season for everything –
a time to be born and a time to die,
a time to plant and a time to uproot . . .
a time to cry and a time to laugh,
a time to grieve and a time to dance.
Ecclesiastes 3:1a, 2, 4

I couldn't understand, Lord,
how you could let it be.
Despite my search for answers,
I simply couldn't see.
Why do we have to suffer?
Why do you let us die?
Why does so much deny you
and give your love the lie?
I've wrestled with such questions
and still not worked them out,
the best that I can offer
a blend of faith and doubt.
Yet in this combination,
this balance of the two,
I'm coming, Lord, to wonder
if there you give a clue.
For just as talk of darkness
demands we speak of light,
so there can be no morning
unless there's also night,
no laughter without sorrow,
no pleasure without pain,

no goodness without evil,
no sunshine without rain.
Unless we have the second
we cannot have the first;
the 'best' has little meaning
unless there is a 'worst'.
Is that what you are saying
as now I grieve in turn?
Is this the vital lesson
you're asking me to learn?
Beginnings go with endings –
I've loved and I have lost.
I've shared such special blessing –
now I must bear the cost.

71

For comfort
in a time of bereavement

I am exhausted by misery;
night after night I soak my bed with tears
and saturate my pillow through my weeping.
Psalm 6:6

'Happy are those who weep', you said;
'happy are they who mourn' –
weeping will turn to joy instead,
pleasure will be reborn;
death will not have the final word,
darkness not win the day,
laughter will once again be heard,
tears will be wiped away.
Help me to trust, Lord, though I grieve,
show me your word is true.
Give me the courage to believe
joy still can shoot anew.
Comfort me in the pain I feel,
order the storm to cease,
reach out in love to help and heal,
come now, and grant your peace.

72

For faith in God's purpose beyond death

I saw a new heaven and earth
in which God will dwell with his people.
He will wipe every tear from their eyes.
There will be no more death
nor any mourning, crying or pain.
Such former things will all have passed away.
Revelation 21:1a, 3b, 4

Give me greater faith, Lord,
in your love that conquers death,
a love that keeps on burning
beyond our dying breath,
a purpose that continues
unchanged for evermore,
and when this life is over
still holds the best in store.
Speak of the special future
you want us to enjoy,
the blessings of your kingdom
that nothing can destroy;
a realm of awesome beauty
where joy will never cease,
no hatred there or warfare,
but everlasting peace;
a place of hope and healing
where tears are washed away,
and those oppressed by darkness
will bask in endless day.

Although my heart is heavy,
although I need to grieve,
Lord, nurture trust within me
and help me to believe.
Remind me truth is greater
than I can comprehend:
however much it seems so,
the grave is not the end.

73
For help in dealing
with the trauma of bereavement

Glory to God, the Father not only
of Jesus Christ our Lord but also of all mercies
– a God full of consolation, who offers us solace
in whatever troubles we are facing.
2 Corinthians 1:3, 4a

I thought that I was ready,
prepared to say goodbye,
aware death waits for no one;
that each of us must die.
I knew loss would be painful,
whatever time it came;
that life from that point onwards
would never be the same,
but even though I feared it,
deep down I dared to hope
that when bereavement hit me
I'd confidently cope.

How different, Lord, the truth
now I'm facing it for real,
how deep the sense of heartbreak
and hopelessness I feel,
how bittersweet the memories,
how bleak the future seems,
how futile all my hoping
and fragile all my dreams.
A world, which seemed so stable,
now whirls in disarray,

for part of me is missing,
for ever plucked away.

Lord, meet me in my sorrow
and grant the help I crave,
remind me of your promise
of life beyond the grave.
Speak of your loving purpose
and help me as I grieve,
to hear your words of comfort
and truly to believe.

74
For greater faith
in God's victory over death

Death has been consumed by victory.
Where is your triumph now, death,
and where is your sting?
1 Corinthians 15:54b, 55

Everything seems diminished,
so much no longer applies;
part of my life feels finished –
death has exacted its prize.
No more will words be spoken,
moments together be shared,
the golden thread is broken
and never can be repaired.
Come, Lord, and grant your healing,
foster contentment anew.
Reach out in love, revealing
all that in time you will do.
Though I may feel forsaken,
bleak though the world might appear,
teach me that I'm mistaken –
show me I've nothing to fear.
Yes, something *is* completed,
but not as so many assume:
death is destroyed, defeated,
life will burst fresh from the tomb!

75

For help in coping with the numbness of bereavement

My eyes grow weary
as I look for the fulfilment of your promise.
'When will you bring me comfort?'
I find myself asking.
Psalm 119:82

Lord, I scarcely dare to face
the pain I feel inside,
running rather from the truth
that one I love has died.
Though I know I need to grieve
before the wounds can heal,
I'm afraid of letting loose
the sense of loss I feel –
scared that I'll be overwhelmed,
engulfed and swept along,
the pent-up tide too fierce to stem,
the memories too strong.

Teach me, Lord, to open up
and bring my fears to you,
trusting you will still the storm
and help me work them through.
So, in time, may I look back
with thanks across the years,

thinking of the days I shared
with joy instead of tears;
confident that though, for now,
death forces us apart,
those I love are with me still,
alive within my heart.

76
For faith
in all God holds in store

We will all be changed, in a flash, in the blink of an eye,
at the last trumpet.
For the trumpet will sound, and the dead will be
raised imperishable, and we will be changed.
For this ephemeral body must put on an eternal body,
and this mortal body must put on immortality.
1 Corinthians 15:51b-53

Speak of your awesome care, Lord,
that death cannot deny,
your sovereign grace and purpose,
your love that will not die.
Comfort me in my sorrow,
breathe peace within my heart,
remind me of the treasures
you promise to impart:
eternal peace and blessing,
unutterable joy,
contentment and fulfilment
that nothing can destroy.
Remind me, when I need it,
that all is not yet done –
a chapter may be over,
but life has just begun.

77

For strength in coping with bereavement

Tears may continue through the hours of darkness,
but joy will come with the dawn.
Psalm 30:5b

How can I cope with this pain inside,
this ache within my heart?
How can I deal with the tears I hide?
Where can I even start?
When will despair loose its stranglehold
and let me find some peace?
When will I laugh as I did of old?
When will the hurting cease?
Part of my life is a part no more,
suddenly gone for good.
Nothing can be as it was before,
much though I wish it could.
Strengthen me, Lord, in this time of need,
comfort me as I mourn.
Reach out your hand to support and lead;
after the night bring dawn.

78
For help and guidance in prayer

One of his disciples said to him,
'Lord, teach us how to pray'.
Luke 11:1

Father, teach me how to pray,
for I don't know what to say,
sometimes so unsure I barely say a word.
Grant me strength to persevere,
keeping faith that you are near
even though it often seems you haven't heard.
Help me share what's deep inside,
doubts and fears I try to hide,
faults and weaknesses I hesitate to name.
Give me faith to bare my soul,
trusting you can make me whole,
set me free from any sense of guilt and shame.
Help me share my hopes and fears,
joy and laughter, pain and tears,
knowing every part of life is your concern.
And to comprehend your will,
teach me also to be still,
so that through your Spirit's prompting I might learn.
Bid me come because I may,
not because I'm told to pray,
but responding to the welcome you extend –
neither nervous nor in dread
but approaching you instead
as a faithful father, living, loving friend.

79

For encouragement
when faith founders

If you appeal to me in prayer, I will hear you;
if you search for me, you will find me;
if you seek me with all your heart,
I will ensure you discover me, says the Lord.
Jeremiah 29:12b-14a

When I find it hard to pray,
troubles seeming here to stay;
dreams in ruins, turned to dust,
sorrow undermining trust,
Lord, be with me, by my side,
be my help, my strength, my guide.
Lead me onwards by your grace,
till I meet you, face to face.

80
For help in practising
what we preach

Not everyone saying to me, 'Lord, Lord'
will enter the kingdom of heaven,
but only those who do the will of my heavenly Father.
Matthew 7:21

Save me from empty pleas, Lord,
from prayers that are short on deeds,
from claiming to care for others
but ignoring their basic needs.
Save me from false religion
through which souls alone are fed –
from faith that offers the gospel
yet forgets to give daily bread.
Fill me with Christ's compassion,
inspire me freely to give,
to share with joy from my plenty
that others might simply live.

81
For help in overcoming our prejudices and preconceptions

There can be neither Jew nor Greek, slave nor free,
male nor female, for you are all one in Jesus Christ.
Galatians 3:28

Lord, for using labels to decide on people's worth:
their age, their sex, their class, their roots,
their faith or place of birth,
their politics or culture, the colour of their skin,
the outward signs that mark them out
instead of what's within;
for summing people up by what nobody can change –
allowing background, creed or race
to poison and estrange –
for all such prejudice, forgive, and from it set me free
to meet the person underneath –
to look and really see.

82
For peace, help and strength

I had become like a broken pot . . .
but you heard my pleas when I cried out for help.
The Lord mends the broken in spirit
and tends their wounds.
Psalm 31:12b, 22b; 147:3

Like a dove come to me, fill me with peace;
Lord, I leave all in your care.
Time now for worry and striving to cease;
always, my God, you are there.
When strength is fading, you heal and renew,
where all seems hopeless, your hand sees me through,
though all else may fail me, your love will stay true:
always, my God, you are there.

Bind up my wounds and in love make me whole;
Lord, I leave all in your care.
Quieten my heart and bring rest to my soul;
always, my God, you are there.
When I am broken you help me rebuild,
with you beside me the turmoil is stilled,
the darkest of moments with light will be filled:
always, my God, you are there.

83

For the transforming touch of God's Spirit

The Spirit generates love, joyfulness, tranquillity,
calmness, compassion, constancy, goodness,
modesty and self-discipline.
Galatians 5:22, 23a

Holy Spirit, gift divine,
come and touch this life of mine.
Give me eyes that I may see.
From my weakness set me free.
Come now, gentle as a dove,
fill my heart with truth and love.

Blow the cobwebs from my soul.
Touch my lips with burning coal.
Cleanse me through your living flame.
Put an end to guilt and shame.
Come as burning tongues of fire,
challenge, comfort, teach, inspire.

Holy Spirit, fall once more,
show me all you hold in store.
Keep my heart from growing cold.
Keep my faith from growing old.
Touch my life like morning dew.
Come, I pray, and make me new.

84
For guidance
in our journey of faith

We have no permanent city here on earth,
but look instead towards the city yet to come.
Hebrews 13:14

Lord, you call me to a journey,
to a never-ending quest,
always seeking new horizons,
always striving for the best.

Young or old, it makes no difference,
still the journey's just begun,
keep me looking in the distance,
for my race is not yet run.

Let my search for truth continue,
may its flame for ever burn –
what I know is only partial,
show me all I need to learn.

Help me hear your voice of challenge,
by your word let me be fed.
Lead, and should I start to wander
help me walk your way instead.

Teach me faith must keep evolving
if it is to stay alive –
though I have a destination
I must travel to arrive.

Lord, you call me to a journey,
always holding one step more.
Help me, then, to keep believing
that you hold the best in store.

85
For guidance
in how and where to serve

For the sake of your name, lead and guide me.
Psalm 31:3b

Lord of life, direct my ways,
help me love you all my days.
Though my faith is flawed and frail,
though I all too often fail,
take my heart, my hands, my feet –
reach out now to all I meet.
Teach me how to serve and when.
Guide my footsteps, Lord. Amen.

86
For help in consecrating our service

The Father will honour all those who serve me.
John 12:26b

Take the life I proffer,
loving God, today;
all the gifts I offer,
all I think and say.
What I am and what I do,
these I give you now.
Lord, I want to serve you –
show me where and how.

87
For help in loving others

If I speak in the tongues of ordinary people
or of angels, but do not have love,
I am nothing more than a blaring trumpet
or a clashing cymbal.
1 Corinthians 13:1

I try so hard to love, Lord,
to reach out in your name;
to know the worst in people
but cherish them the same.
I strive to show compassion,
to show I really care –
yet measured by your goodness
such love cannot compare.
For what I give is partial,
a prize that must be earned;
its constancy dependent
on whether it's returned.
The love you give, in contrast,
is free and unreserved;
poured out with no restrictions,
although it's undeserved.
Lord, come and work within me,
transform my heart of stone,
until the love I offer
grows closer to your own.

88

For an understanding of true riches

Do not amass earthly treasures for yourselves . . .
instead accrue treasures in heaven.
Matthew 6:19a, 20a

In a world awash with greed,
occupied with serving self,
where the overriding creed
honours gain and worships wealth;
where we rarely seem content,
always seeking one thing more,
so much time and effort spent
adding to our worldly store,
gracious Lord, help me to see
where true riches really lie:
show me that your love is free,
something money cannot buy.
Teach me, then, each day to toil
not for treasures of this earth
but for that which will not spoil:
gifts of everlasting worth.

89
For help in hearing God's voice

Do you have eyes, but fail to see?
Do you have ears, but fail to hear?
Mark 8:18

Is this what you're trying to tell me?
Is this what you came to show?
Is this why you left your Father's side
and walked on earth below?
To say, though I often fail you,
and though repeatedly
I let you down and flout your will
and live deceitfully,
despite it all you love me
far more than I can say,
enough to take on human flesh,
and bear it come what may?

Is this what you're trying to tell me,
the truth I need to hear:
the answer to my deepest needs,
to doubt, despair and fear:
that though I may not see it,
and though life can seem bleak,
and though I sometimes strive in vain
to find the joy I seek,
each day you're always waiting
a welcome to extend,
a solid rock when all else fails
on which I can depend?

Is this what you're trying to tell me,
your word of comfort now:
that you will always meet my need
although I can't see how;
that though I'm sometimes puzzled
and often plagued by doubt,
your love will never let me go,
but always seek me out;
that though I overlook you,
and though I lose my way,
your hand will be there just the same
to hold and guide each day?

90

For help in understanding the meaning and cost of <u>discipleship</u>

He said to all, 'If any want to come after me,
let them deny themselves
and take up their cross daily,
and then follow me.
For those wishing to save their life will lose it,
but those who lose their life for my sake
will save it.'
Luke 9:23, 24

How did you feel, Lord Jesus,
when first you heard the call –
when suddenly you realised
you'd give your life for all?
Did you begin to wonder
if you could see it through,
or were you sure already
no other way would do?

How did you feel, Lord Jesus,
when you sat down to dine
and shared with your disciples
a meal of bread and wine?
You knew one would betray you,
and one his faith deny.
How could you still be ready
to give your all and die?

How did you feel, Lord Jesus,
when on the cross you bled –
your body cruelly broken
and thorns pressed on your head?
That cry of 'It is finished!' –
what was it meant to say?
Was it a shout of victory
or protest of dismay?

How did you feel, Lord Jesus,
when, rising from the tomb,
you found the scared disciples
locked in an upper room?
Was that a disappointment,
or did you understand
how hard they must have found it
to grasp your death was planned?

I cannot tell, Lord Jesus,
just what you faced each day;
how much it must have cost you
to walk your chosen way.
But what I need to ponder,
and what you want to know,
is have I heard your challenge
and does my answer show?

INTERCESSION

91
For a world in need

Those in need will not be overlooked for ever,
nor will the dreams of the poor be allowed to die.
When the poor and those in need
look for water but can't find any,
so that their tongues are shrivelled with thirst,
I the Lord God of Israel will answer them;
I will not abandon them.
Psalm 9:18; Isaiah 41:17

In a world of hurt and fear,
teach us, Lord, that you are here.
Come and meet us in our pain;
show that faith is not in vain.
Touch the broken in their grief,
to the troubled bring relief;
grant to all who cannot cope
inner strength, rekindled hope.

In a world awash with need,
scarred by hatred, envy, greed,
come and show how much you care;
foster joy where there's despair.
Hear the pleading of the poor –
lives destroyed by debt and war.
Work to bring new hope to birth,
peace and justice on the earth.

In a world where faith has died,
yet where countless creeds divide,
come and put an end to strife,
all that scars or shatters life.

Heal, renew us, Lord, we pray,
show us where we've gone astray;
give us help to put things right,
turn our darkness into light.

92
For God's healing touch in a troubled world

The Lord is close to those whose hearts are broken
and rescues those who are crushed in spirit.
Psalm 34:18

To all beset by fears,
by sickness, pain or tears,
reach out and make them whole,
in body and in soul.

To all who long for peace,
bid inner turmoil cease;
reach out and touch their life
and put an end to strife.

To all oppressed by care,
regrets, dismay, despair,
reach out and touch their mind;
help put the past behind.

To all who've gone astray,
give light to point the way;
reach out and touch their heart,
your love and life impart.

93
For an awareness
of God's presence
where life is dark

All who sow in tears
will harvest with exclamations of joy.
Those whom the Lord redeems
will return to Zion singing;
eternal ecstasy will rest upon their heads;
they will receive delight and pleasure,
for grief and regret will take flight.
Psalm 126:5; Isaiah 35:10

Where love is met with hatred,
and dreams have been snuffed out,
where days are full of suffering
and faith has turned to doubt,
where evil conquers goodness
and life is full of care,
grant through it all the knowledge
that you, O Lord, are there.

Where joy has turned to sorrow
and hope gives way to fear,
where peace is cruelly shattered
as sudden storms appear,
where life belies convictions
on which we once relied,
grant through it all the knowledge
you're always by our side.

Where darkness like a shadow
extinguishes the light,
where plans are brought to ruin
and nothing quite goes right,
where health begins to falter
and life begins to fade,
grant through it all the knowledge
we need not be afraid.

To those enduring trouble
with which they cannot cope,
to those for whom disaster
has put an end to hope,
to those who carry burdens
too difficult to bear,
grant through it all the knowledge
that you, O Lord, are there.

94
For healing, justice and peace in our world

The Lord seeks the welfare of all and justice
for those who are exploited.
He rescues the needy when they call,
the poor and those who have no one else to help them.
Psalm 72:12; 103:6

Hear my prayer for others
in the trials they face –
fellow sisters, brothers:
grant to all your grace.
Heal the crushed and broken,
body, mind and soul –
let your word be spoken,
touch and make them whole.

Chide the rich and greedy,
strengthen the oppressed,
reach out to the needy,
comfort the distressed.
May the humble flourish
may the poor be fed,
in your mercy nourish
all who crave for bread.

Bring to every nation
harmony once more,
reconciliation,
peace instead of war.
Hear my intercession,
make my life a prayer;
help me give expression
to your love and care.

95

For real and lasting change

Wash and make yourselves clean.
Take your evil deeds out of my sight!
Stop doing wrong, learn to do right!
Seek justice, encourage the oppressed.
Defend the cause of the fatherless.
Plead the case of the widow.
Isaiah 1:16, 17

An urgent voice is calling,
a voice from far away;
it's crying out for justice,
and yearning for that day
when no one need go hungry,
despair will be no more –
a day at last that heralds
a new start for the poor.

An urgent voice is calling,
a voice from somewhere near;
it's crying out with longing,
yet no one seems to hear;
despite long years of witness,
a multitude still search –
forgive me, Lord, and grant now
a new start for the Church.

An urgent voice is calling,
a voice from all around;
it's crying out in anguish,
the grim and tragic sound

of God's creation groaning,
stripped bare, denied her worth –
Lord, curb my greed, and bring now
a new start for the earth.

An urgent voice is calling,
a voice from close at hand;
it's crying out in anger,
campaigning for a land
where all will be respected,
and war will find no place –
a world of peace and friendship,
a new start for our race.

An urgent voice is calling,
the voice of God above;
it's crying out in sorrow,
and urging me to love,
for still a world lies bleeding,
the weak go to the wall –
Lord, help us build with others
a new start for us all.

96

For reconciliation in a divided world

How good and precious it is
when people live together in unity.
Psalm 133:1

Lord, to our world in its madness –
broken, bemused and concussed,
crushed by a burden of sadness,
ravaged by fear and mistrust –
grant your renewal and healing,
courage where hope seems in vain,
reach out to all who are reeling,
bring them relief from their pain;
break down the roots of division,
walls that destroy and estrange;
overcome hate and suspicion,
grant us the prospect of change.

97

For the elderly and infirm

Our life expectancy is seventy years,
if we're lucky,
and of that fleeting span a large part
brings trial and tribulation.
Our years fly past, and life races by in tandem.
Psalm 90:10

Reach out to those who are ageing,
all for whom life is a strain,
those who are constantly waging
war against illness and pain.
Comfort the troubled and tearful,
give them your help to get by.
Strengthen those worried and fearful,
lovingly answer their cry.

Nurture the broken and ailing –
bodies grown weary and old,
faculties steadily failing –
scared what the future might hold.
Help those who, friendless and lonely,
wish that each day were their last,
those who find happiness only
when thinking of moments long past.

Lord, though the years lead to testing,
often too bitter to bear,
leaving some sadly protesting,

feeling you no longer care,
show that the future's not finished,
that your love still offers more,
carrying on undiminished,
holding the best things in store.

98

For those who care enough to show it

Isn't this the fast I want from you:
to untie the knots of evil,
to undo the straps of the yoke,
to allow the exploited freedom,
and to break every form of oppression?
Isn't it to share your bread with the hungry
and offer hospitality to the homeless;
to clothe the naked when you see them,
and not to turn your back
on your own flesh and blood?
Isaiah 58:6, 7

For those who fight injustice
and make a stand for good,
who strive to give the poor a chance
to live life as they should,
for all who labour, heart and soul,
to make our world more fair,
I ask your courage, succour, strength –
Lord, answer, hear my prayer.

For those who show compassion,
who work to heal and mend,
who nurse the sick, support the weak,
encourage and befriend,
for all who reach out in your name
to offer love and care,
I ask your blessing, power, help –
Lord, answer, hear my prayer.

For those who tackle conflict,
where wounds run red and raw,
who strive to conquer hatred
and put a stop to war,
who work to foster dialogue
despite the scars we bear,
I ask your guidance, vision, faith –
Lord, answer, hear my prayer.

For those who try to witness
to Christ through word and deed,
to show his love embraces
each colour, culture, creed,
who point to light and life and hope
in which we all can share,
I ask your wisdom, grace and truth –
Lord, answer, hear my prayer.

99

For those struggling to come to terms with questions of faith

Why do you let me witness wrongdoing
and endure trouble? Destruction
and aggression are all around me;
conflicts and disputes spring up everywhere.
The law is watered down
such that justice has no chance of winning through.
Habakkuk 1:3, 4a

Lord, I see such goodness,
yet such evil too:
much that makes me question,
much that speaks of you.
All around are riddles
hard to understand –
help me find some answers,
help me see your hand.

Where there's pain and sorrow,
where your children bleed,
where there seems no future
for a world in need,
break into the darkness,
bring an end to night,
show that love continues,
shine again your light.

Where belief is shaken,
hope appearing vain,
where reserves are creaking,
sorely under strain,
grant the strength to trust you,
courage to hold out;
show us you are present;
speak, Lord, in our doubt.

100
For a world
in which God seems absent

Tears are my food day and night,
while people keep on saying to me,
'Where is your God?'
Psalm 42:3

Where were you, Lord, when the planes struck
and the towers came crashing down?
What did you do to stop it?
Why were you out of town?
Where were you in the Balkans
when the streets ran red with blood?
And how about the shanty town
engulfed by streams of mud?
Why don't you end the famine?
Why don't you stop the war?
How can you let these happen?
What can it all be for?

Lord, is it wrong to ask you,
faithless to speak my mind?
Shouldn't I look for answers?
Don't you say 'seek and find'?
Yes, I know much is beyond me,
truth often hard to discern,
but I'm ready and willing to listen,
eager and hungry to learn.
Don't think I'm daring to judge you,
set myself up in your place –

some things, I know, must stay hidden,
at least till we meet face to face –
yet in a world where so many
feel faith and hope are in vain,
give us some sign, Lord, I beg you
to prove you are here in our pain.

101
For those under the shadow of <u>death</u>

Blessed are those who mourn;
they will be comforted.
Matthew 5:4

Lord, I pray for those who weep,
mourning those they've loved and lost;
happiness that ran so deep
followed now by such a cost;
each day bringing added pain,
memories of times they knew,
never to be shared again –
life a case of getting through.
When their hearts are fit to break –
hurt too bitter to express –
grant them solace, dull the ache,
comfort them in their distress.
In their anger, loss and shock,
help them find in you a friend;
in their turmoil be their rock,
one on whom they can depend.
Though they feel they cannot cope,
gracious God, reach out to save;
bring to each new life, new hope
in your love, beyond the grave.

102
For signs of God's kingdom here on earth

Then I saw a new heaven and earth;
for the first heaven and earth,
together with the sea,
had come to an end.
There will be no more night,
nor need of any light from a lamp or the sun,
for the Lord God will be their light,
and they will reign for evermore.
Revelation 21:1; 22:5

Grant, Lord, an end to our sorrow,
a halt at last to our pain,
the hope of a brighter tomorrow,
of sunshine, after the rain.
Assure us the day is dawning
when darkness will be no more,
no suffering, dying or mourning,
no violence, hatred or war –
a kingdom of joy unbounded,
of laughter, blessing and peace,
where evil will be confounded
and all divisions cease;
a time of celebration,
a place of rare delights –
Lord, finish your new creation
and set our world to rights.

103
For ourselves, the Church and the world

Above all, therefore, I would advocate that you offer
requests, intercessions and thanksgiving
in your prayers for everyone.
1 Timothy 2:1

Take this day, I ask you, Lord,
fashion all that it shall bring;
help me see your hand at work,
love transforming everything.

Take my life, I ask you, Lord,
through your Spirit make me new;
help me now to do your will,
trusting you in all I do.

Take your Church, I ask you, Lord,
grant it strength to meet your call;
help it show through word and deed
something of your love for all.

Take our world, I ask you, Lord,
may its pain and sorrow cease;
help us heal each other's wounds,
show us how to live in peace.

104
For the Church

I pray for all those who will believe in me . . .
that they may all be one, as we are one,
I living in them as you live in me,
in order that they may become so completely united
that the world is left in no doubt that you sent me
and love them, as you have loved me.
John 17:20b, 21b, 23

You've called us as your Church, Lord,
your people here on earth,
a fellowship of equals
where all are given worth,
a family together,
distinguished by our care,
one faith, one hope, one gospel,
one vision that we share.
Yet we have been divided
by doctrine, dogma, creed,
estranged from one another –
we've left your wounds to bleed.
Too full of our convictions,
believing others wrong,
we've lost sight of the body
to which we all belong.
Our differences deny you,
betray the faith we claim;
instead of love uniting,
we squabble in your name.
Lord, heal the wounds that scar us –
suspicion, fear and pride;

reveal the good in others
that all our labels hide.
May cords of love unite us,
too strong to be undone –
although we may be many,
equip us to be one.

Index of Bible readings

(references relate to poem rather than page numbers)

Index of themes

(references relate to poem rather than page numbers)